Yarrow and Smoke

YARROW AND SMOKE

WILLIAM O'DALY

Folded Word
Meredith, New Hampshire

ISBN: 978-1-61019-241-5

Folded Word
79 Tracy Way
Meredith, NH 03253
United States of America
FOLDED.WORDPRESS.COM

This book is dedicated to
Sam Hamill and Galen Garwood,
my brothers on the long, narrow road

Contents

Preface

The earliest of these poems had its origin around a small, bottomland fire, where late one summer night a friend and I sat catfishing along the Tuolumne River. The most recent poem emerged from a painting by Gary Edward Foster, of a crane dancing, its wings spread, which I came across at the Sacramento Fine Arts Center and which found its final form in rehearsal with a group of young, talented jazz musicians. Both were written in California's Central Valley, one hundred miles and forty years apart.

During the intervening decades, I made a loop through the upper Western United States, through the harmonic and the cacophonic—the mundane, the wondrous, the painful, and the beautiful. I lived a life I would never have imagined, a life which fueled my intuition and provided me with what I needed to learn. Running through *Yarrow and Smoke* are mysteries and revelations from that long journey, what I value and what I seek.

But it wasn't me who discovered the underlying currents that make up this small book. JS Graustein, editor in chief of Folded Word, proposed the gathering and its sequence. For Ms. Graustein and her family, for editor Rose Auslander and the entire Folded Word staff, I am grateful. And none of this would have come to pass were it not for my loved ones, family and friends, for those I miss terribly and those who light each day.

~ *William O'Daly*

Acknowledgments

Mr. O'Daly would like to thank the staff of the following publications and presses for their support of his poems by including previous versions in their journals and books:

"Catfishing"
   The Portland Review, Vol. 23, 1977; awarded Student Award by judge Vern Rutsala.

"Our Names Returning After Rain"
   Copperhead (broadside), 1976; *Portland Review,* Vol. 23, 1977; *hardpan,* Spring 2006; *Oregon Literary Review,* audio, 2009; adapted to lyrics by the jazz group iiii and included on their debut album, *iiii,* 2013.

"Living Legend"
   Valley Grapevine, 1978

"After the Drought"
   Susurrus, Guest Writer, Spring 2011, print.

"The Fire"
   Willow Springs, Issue 14, Spring 1986.

"Legacy"
Susurrus, Guest Writer, Spring 2011, print.

"The Ruins"
RATTLE, Issue 34, Winter 2010, print.

"Monday"
Medusa's Kitchen, January 14, 2011, online.

"Heron Dances Over the World"
Life and Legends, Inaugural Issue, Summer 2014;
Sacramento Voices, Cold River Press (anthology),
2014.

"Civilization"
Great River Review, Spring-Summer 2013.

The author and publisher thank Rose Auslander for
her editorial efforts in expediting the publication of
this book. They also thank Zakariah Johnson, Casey
Tingle, Barbara Flaherty, Kristine Slentz, Sarah
Gibson, Claire Graustein, Ian Graustein, and Kurt
Graustein for their assistance at the press during its
production.

YARROW AND SMOKE

CATFISHING

The black river sleeps.
On my palms, the smell
of embalmed bait lingers.
I rub damp clay
and dream a strike. Firelight.
Beached cans and bottles wait
for the next big rain.

A long industrial drone—
coots grumble across the water.
Canneries steam back streets—
the shift swings to graveyard.
Diesels. Horns and sirens
howl down the blood.

My fire's reflection
on this starless river—
the harvest moon snagged
deep in burning roots.

Our Names Returning After Rain

After a night of talk
beside a wavering fire,
we walk the bottomland road
and count the stars still sputtering.
One by one their bright names trail
down the fields of tender light
into a green sea of vines.
Lichen graze flat stones
once sidearmed across
the river's surface.
These all bear names
we raise to fruition—
rain also is of the process.

Under the charred trestle
we carve our given names,
our lives—the cut fingers
of children late for school.
We wrap each other
in the pure white of absence,
bloom crimson,

                darker.
Together we begin.

Wind blows through the burnt oak
but forgets from where it came,
forgets what to call the rain,
as we, opening our mouths
to speak what we are,
forget who we have been.

Living Legend

Slumped shoulders, baggy trousers,
flat brown hat, blue hyacinth eyes blooming
on the backlot paths you scuffle
down, bearing
your catch wrapped in newsprint,
barter at Lee Sung's market.

You rise where the black sun
greases the rheumatic river
and kicks over the breeze.
You clip the Baptists' lawn,
trim the Holy Rollers' hedge.
Walnuts loosen themselves
where river towns used to be.
Old Relic, will there be blight?
Tell me again about being a boy
riding the last wheat train
over fresh track, the long team of Arabians
hitched to the reaper that mesmerized you.
Tell me the stories of antelope and wildflowers
your father made up to lull you to sleep,
of dust storms sent as penance.
Evenings when you shut your door
on a city unable to see you
the magpies scrape the tin roof,
distant neon blisters your window.

Striking up the two-burner
electric stove, boil water for nettle,
heat the skillet for stew.
A bare bulb hisses a prayer.
The mirror reflects nothing.
At the table in a halo of light
our hands separate the bones
to be thrown into the sacred holes
where young catfish chase the moon
like orphans berserk with whiteness.
Down by the river, ghosts of brothers
huddle around a broken ring of stones,
each refusing to speak the name of she
who used his labor for profit
and his madness for love.

Asleep on your mattress, Catfish,
you turn toward the wall.
Above the Tuolumne, the jasmine
singes the night air and those vacant stars
that were the eyes of god
whistle with the wind.
You turn again, roused
by the faraway cracks of .22s,
as mudhens, bushes, trees
all freeze on the still river.
Your burlap pouch of sardines
hangs in the old walnut tree
waiting for morning, for sunlight
to glisten on the face
of the hole cut deep into the bank,
on the tangled roots of its roof,
on the leaves swirling above,
on the silver bait
that'll lure the cats home
one more time.

AFTER THE DROUGHT

for Dale McGowan

The frozen bells
of Catedral San Joaquin
clang this gray valley awake.
We drink together,
rethink our worth in rain,
epitaphs written by gales.
The heavy drops carry
a year of dust down the window.
Old walnut branches bleed at the cuts,
the cherry sapling we planted
patiently waits for spring.
Your ex-wife phones
to say the roof leaks,
and your daughter's faint voice
leaps into your arms. We salute
the feeble river, the grass taking a first breath.
Later you can tell her the sun
isn't this land's love.

THE TURNING YEAR

Here is a place to raise our cups—
where last spring we perched on a boulder
still warm from all day sun, and cast
our lines into the moonlit river.
Late thaw tumbled and whitened
beyond what is known of thunder,
of time slipping from the pools below.
Through the grasslands and gorge,
you cleared a switchback trail
five hundred miles in my blood.
All summer, moist light spun
the leaves and purple clusters.
Then yellow mountain ash.

Home at last, you sip wine
beneath the naked mimosa
and drift near sleep,
beyond flood leveled plains
and the snowy mountains between us.
This casual moonlight holds you, holds me,
where we are. Even far apart
we share everything—the deep red wine
of some distant summer
and the harvest moon
floating in our cups.

THE FIRE

Sunlight spins a web
among young pines,
migratory ferns, red columbine,
over Rock Creek tumbling
from a cloud hidden peak
and down this mountainside
to fill the ocean; moss hangs
from the madrone like the tails
of grazing horses that'll rear up
and step into a final gallop
should the sparrows ignite.

Seven days of hiking
switchback passes
that connect a chain of glacial lakes,
weary in our muscles and thought,
we step down rock
after granite rock,
into the body of summer
and a buzzing like memory
among the grass of Parnassus.
Water splashes below us, aluminum
cups jangle against the packs,
we climb in the descent
and our breathing deepens—
trails fork or wash out,
scrabbling over scree
and fallen pine
to rejoin the creek.

Dipping our cups, we
catch a whisper,
we are breath,
exhalations who live
our full moment
and later as pigment, a layer
of red clay in the mountain.
Days ago, our names began
to read like trails
that never arrive—
a night wind seeped
through the tent walls
and collected in our mouths,
tasting of yarrow and smoke.

Our prayer is the sweat souring
creases of elbows and clothes,
these trembling limbs,
and later the silence
only questions sustain.

Farther on, stopping to cool
our blistered feet in the water,
we both for no reason recalled
how in fifth grade, when
the whole class had been bad,
the teacher explained
that in the unlikely event
of an official accident
at an inland reactor, or
because we live in a state
of strategic importance,
our hormones could be
separated from matter.
Our bones, like skeletons
of horses or of history,
torn from our souls
and released as vapor.

The excesses of light recede,
and shadows grow
across the creek. In your hand,
the knife joins
dried fish and bread, bread and wild onion:
we are born again when a seed
splits inside us,
in the conch where blood
sounds its salty praise
for what we make possible tonight.

A breeze freshens—we wake
to snowmelt and salt lingering
on the tongue, to the eyes of a deer
shining among the hemlock,
and a mile farther down, a nighthawk diving
at the edge of alder trees.

The trail levels and widens
under the highway, then evaporates
in cool sand. Gulls squabble
over a last scrap of rotten clam,
and we trudge past shallow pools,
slipping the packs from our backs
to kiss the ebbing sea.

Driftwood flares up, consumes
the borders of our bodies
in a widening circle of light,
where elbow to elbow we sit
with inner ears tuned to the cry
of burning cities, two losses held hostage
on the stem. Could clasped hands
preserve the common world,
we might break the charge
of that final death, tumbling in
from the black sea. We listen
to the wind—horses disappear
midstride in the mind;
a black seed sleeps
in the unborn child's name.

It's happening at home, and on the
    northern peninsula—
neighbors who live on clearcut bluffs
turn out the lamps every night
in a wave. We have no country
to escape to: they say when we enter
the violet gates of heaven,
the body flames
in a marriage of spirit and action
so close to pure purpose
every word blossoms erotic.

Dark rocks glint in the moon's tide,
an image of us burns
through my eyes, over the treetops
in the spine of a northerly.
You and I are lost in darkness,
lying under separate stars,
at the edge of firelight.

LEGACY

Grandfather, these inland hills
and the canyons we blasted with .22s
shrink in the August sun.
Housing tracts put a stop
to our bullets; at night streetlights climb
like the edge of a wave
over sage crowded slopes.
Stones embroider *Vista del Mar*
among the poppies, where cars pass
the guard and through the gates.
At long tables, buyers peruse
the shuffle of hacienda façades
fifty miles from the nearest sea.
Hawks are few; they circle the bones
of banks under construction,
the air-conditioned curios
with "Country" in their names.
But on the ridge, the cottage you built
with your hands and knotty pine
has sold and sold again,
grown to twice its size. The prickly pear
out back follows suit, and in the narrow canyon
boulders bear the scars of all our bullets,
and the winds call us home
across the forgotten stream bed
that was never ours.

THE RUINS

Neither cloud nor dream can exist in words—
not even the olive tree, silvery,
and in winter, slate blue. The light of
an extinguished star no longer guides
our destiny—indivisible—
even as it empties the sky.
Navigating by the rose, we steer
without pause through the burning ruins.
But when we speak our truth, the children
swarm the station, bothering
the frightened passengers. You're not old,
the stone steps to South Heaven Gate
and the trains are old, and now we can see
the songs too are ancient. I'm not partial
to romantic love, to politics or speeches,
and even if God designed the cathedral and the
    shark,
we, like the wave, eventually will empty.
So, what do you say—
shall we give the earth back to our feet?

    after Odysseas Elytis

FAIRY TALE

So what will I do when
my book goes to seed?

Plant it and grow
another pumpkin?

Or impart the words with coffee
and turn them to cinders.

MONDAY

The rising sky
holds the light
of a windblown star.

Time has always
been this way. This blue.
Or *this* blue?

I spit out the bone—
all that remains
is the sacred.

Four Moments

MAP

Strands of web linger
in the branches, a bee stirs,
and the tangled shadows
promise a world without grief.

Bird

Every word, thicket, and stone
in this fractured stand of aspen—
living chord, sonata, a single cry—
settle the misty mountain peaks.

The Quiet Hills

Yellow moon rises
above the sugar pine
in the endless sky—
ten thousand crickets.

SUMMER

Crows chase a raccoon
along the wooden fence—
into the silence of a sunlit yard.

HERON DANCES OVER THE WORLD

Even you're not watching
as you spread your black tattered wings
and step among the colors of the physical world—
spindly legs conjure the symbol for infinity
in red earth, in fresh blue snow and white mist.

Endangered islands bloom, the wetland fills
with mountain shadow. In a parallel universe
your reflection moves to its inner calling,
to folded granite, music of the waterfall.

You live as hidden origami, with creases
and abandon, intricate patterns that resist
the receding shore. You circle like an equation
neither eyes nor lips can touch—motion that can't
    be solved
or written on the tongue. You do not stop to preen
among the battered dunes.

Your cry wrings iron from irony,
recalls the silent bells, laments the love
I've forgotten. You breathe closer to the swaying
    aspen
than to the orphaned moon and the tide's pull.

In this dance you create like a beetle
your own being. You become possibility.

To Fabulous Liars and the Truth

for Doug Jarman

From the first call to the music of an evening
in the Sonoran hills, your feet like fire
dance to Mack the Knife along the cantina's bar,
lighting the notes that migrate from down under
to the deepening sky, born and sung in this
season of wings. My friend, imagine, with our
    hands,
with passion and wanting we built this life—
so right and today secret, long-gone dreams of
shaggy-haired rockers, left under a sun that
blisters even the young. How can it be we've
known each other so long? Who knows
where we will be a hundred years
from today? No answer but laughter
singeing our hands and our feet,
our throats open to the falling stars.

CIVILIZATION

Jackhammers and saws, pitchforks and blowers,
uneasy sounds of commuters boarding the train,
metaphor allegedly lost when the library burned—
the gate and the fountain, the bomb and the knife,
the poem preserved as smoke, under layers of ash.

About the Author

WILLIAM O'DALY has translated eight books of the late-career and posthumous poetry of Chilean Nobel laureate Pablo Neruda, and most recently Neruda's first volume, *Book of Twilight* — all published by Copper Canyon Press. His books of poems include *The Whale in the Web,* published by Copper Canyon Press, as well as *The Road to Isla Negra* and *Water Ways* (a collaboration with JS Graustein), both published by Folded Word. A National Endowment for the Arts Fellow, William was a finalist for the 2006 Quill Award in Poetry and was profiled by Mike Leonard for *The Today Show.* He has received national and regional honors for literary editing and instructional design, and was a national board member of Poets Against War. Most recently he was awarded by the State of California for his work on the California Water Plan.

To learn more, please visit his website:
WILLIAMODALY.COM

About the Press

Since 2008, Folded Word has been
exploring the world, one voice at a time
with the help of editors, authors, and readers
who value sustainable literature.

For a complete list of our titles, visit the Folded
Word website: FOLDED.WORDPRESS.COM

To report typographical errors, email:
FOLDEDEDITORS@GMAIL.COM

Want more information about our titles? Want to
connect with our authors? No problem. Simply join
us at a social media outlet near you:

- Facebook: www.facebook.com/foldedword
- Twitter: twitter.com/foldedword

FOLDED WORD IS A PROUD MEMBER OF

[clmp]

Community of Literary Magazines and Presses
Ensuring a vibrant, diverse literary landscape
www.clmp.org

AND GIVES ANNUAL SUPPORT TO:

Poets House
*A place for poetry: library, literary center,
locus of poetic inspiration*
poetshouse.org

The Haiku Foundation
*Preserving and archiving the first century of haiku in
English; providing resources for the next*
www.thehaikufoundation.org

WHAT DID YOU THINK?

☆ ☆ ☆ ☆ ☆

Let us know with a quick rating or review at
GoodReads.com
or wherever you search for books.

Folded Word reserves a portion of each print
run to donate to libraries and reading programs
in under-served communities. Please email us at
FoldedEditors@gmail.com if you would like your
organization to be considered.

This book and its cover were designed and typeset by JS Graustein. The cover features the artwork "Plains of Leuctra" by Galen Garwood.

The title face is Freight Sans Pro, designed by Joshua Darden in 2009, issued by GarageFonts.

Supplemental glyphs are ornaments of Poetica, designed by Robert Slimbach in 1992, issued by Adobe Systems.

The text face is Garamond Premier Pro, designed by Robert Slimbach in 2007, issued by Adobe Systems.

CPSIA information can be obtained
at www.ICGtesting.com
Printed in the USA
LVHW111739280419
615868LV00001B/57/P